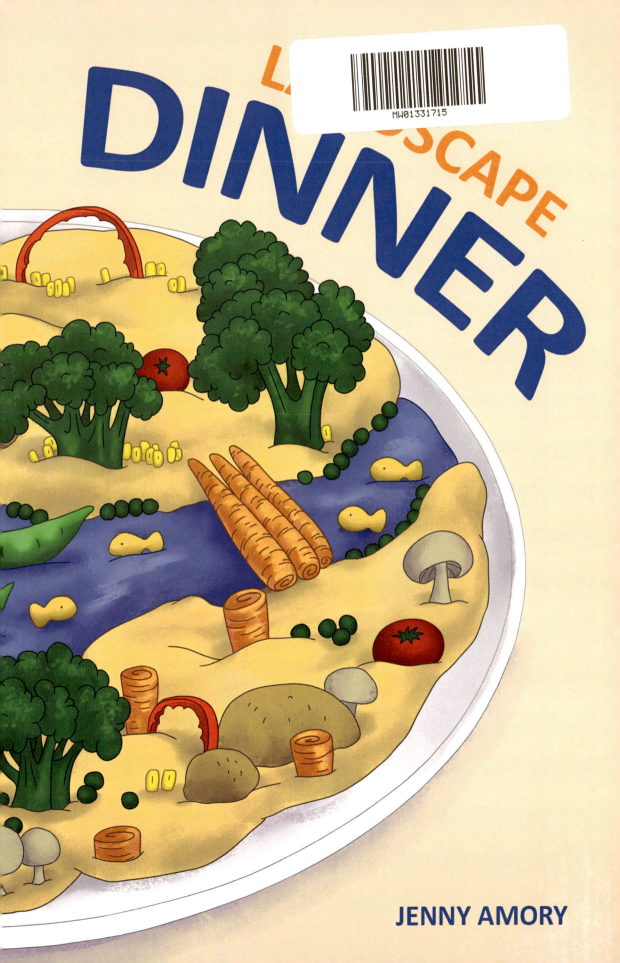

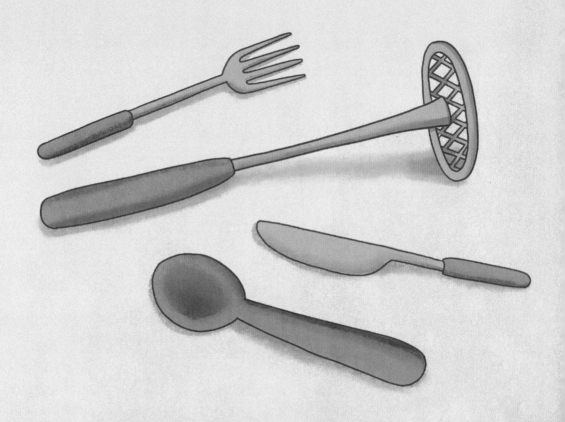

Landscape Dinner

©2020 by Jenny Amory. All rights reserved. No part of this publication may be reproduced or transmitted in any form or by any means, electronic or mechanical, without written permission by the author.

Credits:

Written by Jenny Amory

Illustrated by Emiliya Iskrenova

Edited by Sarah Jane Shangraw

Printed by KDP, an Amazon.com company

Dedicated to Jeremy and Kyle, my two amazing sons, and to Bill and Joan, my incredible parents, and my loving partner, John.

Jeremy and I were playing soccer when Mommy came running outside and said, "Are you ready?"
At the same time, we said, "For what?"

"To make a special dinner only you can make," she said.

I looked at Jeremy and he looked at me. What could Mommy be talking about?

"Follow me into the kitchen."

Wow, you should have seen the kitchen! There were bowls of mashed potatoes colored blue, carrots, and corn on the cob.

I saw Goldfish crackers peeking at us. . .

and a circle of broccoli lining the plate.

Mommy said, "We are going to make a landscape dinner."

Jeremy and I looked at each other again. We exclaimed at the same time, "What is a landscape dinner?"

"First, I'm going to take the blue mashed potatoes and make a lake."

Mommy used a wooden spoon to plop and spread mashed potatoes in a circle on a platter.

"Then I'm going to put some fish in the lake because they need a place to swim."

She put Goldfish in the potatoes. We started to giggle and soon we were laughing.

Jeremy put carrots across the potatoes to make a bridge over the blue lake.

Jeremy said, "Look, Kyle, I can make the broccoli stand up like trees next to mushroom boulders."

I made dirt from stuffing and created a path from the lake to the broccoli trees. I laughed as my fingers got sticky.

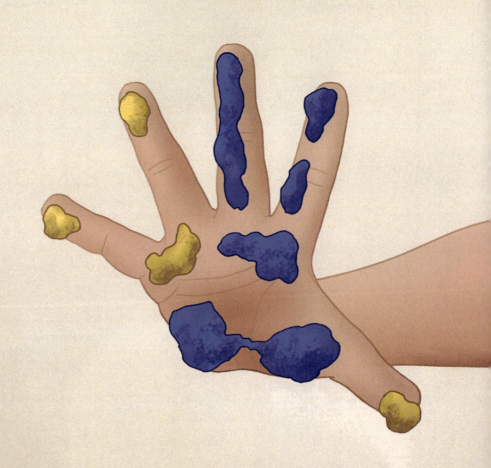

After we finished our landscape, we ate the dinner that we had created, all the while laughing and laughing.

What foods would your family use

to create a landscape dinner?

Made in the USA
Middletown, DE
18 January 2023

22363455R00020